THE PAINTED HOME

BY *Dena*™

THE
PAINTED
HOME

BY *Dena*™

PHOTOGRAPHS BY
JOHN ELLIS

STEWART, TABORI & CHANG
NEW YORK

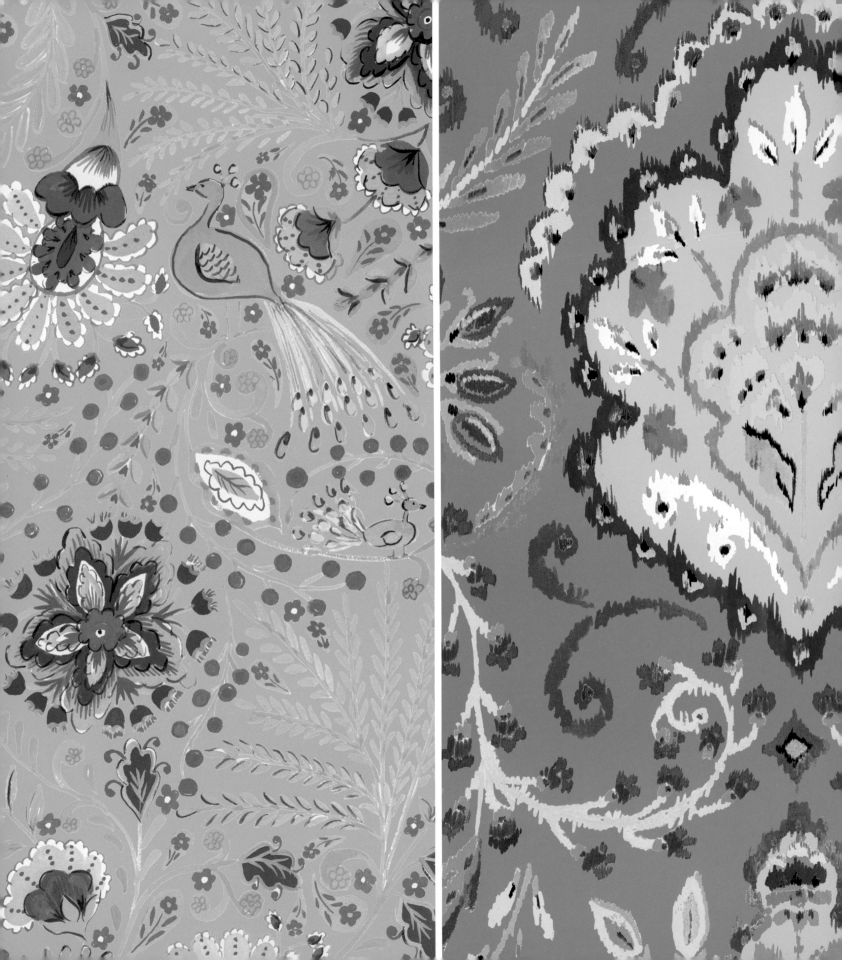

Contents

INTRODUCTION

Surround Yourself with the Things You Love

What makes a house a home? *It is truly the memories of our life that make that distinction.*

Our house, which we've lived in for almost eighteen years, is far more than just a house. It provides shelter, but it also feeds our senses and nurtures our spirits. Just before we moved in, I was given the book *Living a Beautiful Life* by Alexandra Stoddard. One of the main messages of her book is to live even the most ordinary of days as a celebration. I took that sentiment to heart and translated it to my home as I designed and redesigned

each room. Even the most mundane of spaces should be as exuberant and as filled with life and love as you can manage. Now, when we walk through our rooms, we feel good—each one, in its own way, reflects who we are and what we care about in life.

I hope that with this book you'll be motivated by that very principle and use the many photos, designs, and projects I've included as inspiration in making your own home.

A home has a heart. It's a place where you want to be, a place that you want to share, and a place in which memories are made. It's the setting for gatherings of all shapes and sizes, from family dinners to holiday celebrations, from a child's birthday party to tea with a friend. As you make your house your home, it's important to consider the function of each space, whether it's communal or private, and the feeling it gives: The kitchen should be practical yet warm and welcoming; dining areas should be equally suited to eating and conversation; family and living rooms should be comfortable and delightful; bedrooms should be havens for relaxing and dreaming; guest rooms should have all the amenities possible to ensure their inhabitants feel cared for and at ease.

As an extension of who you are, your home should reflect your personality and what you and your family care about most in life. Buying basic furniture and accessories is the way many of us get started, but individualizing generic purchases with personal touches is what gives your home its unique character and warmth. There are countless simple and inexpensive ways to transform what may be plain or everyday into something special. With a trip to the flea market, a little paint, a needle and thread, a glue gun, a yard of beautiful fabric . . . there's no limit to what you can do.

Creating a home is a journey. As you go, think about what you need from a practical standpoint but also what will bring pleasure to you, your family, and your guests. Pay attention to the details. Think about color and pattern, about the things that you want to look at and enjoy on a daily basis. Maybe it's fresh-cut flowers, a bowl filled with beautiful shells or fresh Meyer lemons. Stay open to anything that piques your imagination. A swatch of vintage fabric may inspire a fabric-covered wall, a lovely pillow, or a hand-painted lampshade. As with any great journey, half the fun is in the unexpected.

This book is about creating a home that brings you joy and happiness. It offers up inexpensive ideas for embellishing everyday rooms and objects, for cultivating an environment that's both beautiful and comfortable, and for drawing inspiration from places you may not have thought to look. In the pages to come, I share photographs of our home, anecdotes and style notes, along with many ideas for simple, inexpensive projects you can do yourself. There's even a stencil so you can get started right away.

I hope you'll use this book as a jumping off point. Start small, and take the time you need to plan your journey. Work one step at a time, and don't be afraid to make mistakes. When it comes to purchases and projects, follow your heart and trust your instincts. Don't forget to involve your family in decisions that will affect them . . . and most importantly, surround yourself with the things you love, and your home will be a place that you—and those you love—want to be.

Our living room is one of our most formal spaces, yet it's as inviting and comfortable as any room in our home.

Opposite: An eclectic combination of flea market finds and handmade touches gives our sunroom its personality.

Left: Fresh-cut flowers bring the lovely color and feel of the garden into the house.

Right: I love pillows. They provide comfort and a splash of color.

WELCOME TO SEVEN OAKS RANCH

ENTRYWAY AND FAMILY ROOM

ENTRYWAY

I've always believed it's not what you say that matters as much as how you say it and the way you make people feel when you're talking to them. The same can be said of your home: When someone visits, you want them to feel good, welcome, and at ease. If your house is relaxed, they'll be relaxed. If you're content and happy in your space, others will be, too.

The entryway sets the tone. Ours is a sunny yellow. I knew that I wanted the walls to be a warm, inviting color, but it took me some time to figure out the rest. When I decorate, I often work a step at a time. In this room, I painted the background color first and lived with it for a while. A month or so later, I decided to add the vines, leaves, and flowers. I love painting vine patterns because they are free-form; they do take some practice, but it's lovely to sketch the design and not need to make sure everything is perfect and evenly spaced.

Working in stages takes the pressure off. The beauty of this method is you don't have to do everything at once—nor does every project have to be huge. When a partial idea comes to you, go with it! If you're not sure what to do next, let go for a bit. If you discover you don't like what you've done, you can add more or take away—later. When it comes to decorating, remember that most things can be changed easily.

Simple, thoughtful touches—whether purchased or homemade—reveal who you are and what's important to you. In our entryway, family and friends are greeted by colorful details. The delicate tole chandeliers are flea market finds; we have a set of two we found years apart but they are a perfect match. The cheerful assortment of hand-sewn pillows and the pretty porcelain plates add color and pattern. Like the opening of a garden path, this space is practical, yet inviting. It's a point of entry . . . and a hint of what's to come.

Salt-and-Pepper-Shaker Tassels

Add some vintage charm to your curtains, your Christmas tree, or the key to an armoire! Salt-and-pepper-shaker tassels can be used to embellish all sorts of things.

GATHER:

Wire cutters

26-gauge wire

Salt shaker and pepper shaker, preferably vintage

Beads in a variety of sizes

Glue gun and glue sticks

Fabric adhesive, such as Fabri-Tac

1 yard cotton bullion fringe

Small-tipped scissors

Variety of decorative trims

CREATE:

1. Cut a piece of wire about 12 inches long. Thread the wire into the hole at the bottom of the salt shaker and then up through one of the holes at the top. Leave a 4-inch tail of wire at the bottom of the shaker.

2. Thread a small bead (one that won't slip into the shaker hole), a medium bead, a large bead, and another medium bead onto the wire at the top of the shaker. Continue to thread tiny beads onto the wire until you have enough to create a loop.

3. Thread a large bead onto the wire, then insert the end of the wire into the other hole at the top of the shaker and back down through the bottom hole. Both ends of the wire should now be coming through the bottom hole.

4. Twist the two wire ends together until the beaded loop is held firmly in place.

5. Trim the ends and use a glue gun to adhere them to the bottom of the shaker.

6. Place a line of Fabri-Tac along the top edge of the bullion fringe, then roll the fringe up tightly. Continue rolling the fringe until it is the same diameter as the bottom of the shaker, making a perfect tassel.

7. Use a glue gun to adhere the tassel to the bottom of the shaker.

8. Use a glue gun to adhere decorative trim around the top of the tassel where it meets the shaker. Add additional trim as desired.

9. Loop a small piece of trim through the beaded loop to hang.

10. Repeat with the pepper shaker.

EYE CANDY

From a choice, one-of-
a-kind piece to a quirky
collection, wow your guests
with something that's fun
and interesting.

SET THE TONE

Establish whatever style or feeling you want to evoke in the entryway, where visitors get their first impression of you and your home.

Right: A cheerful pile of homemade pillows seems to say, "Come in, sit down, and make yourself at home!"

Opposite: Danny and I found this vintage tole chandelier at the flea market.

Reverse Appliqué Pillow

Reverse appliqué is a fun and easy sewing technique that can be used to make the prettiest of pillows.

GATHER:

Fabric pencil

Store-bought solid-colored pillow cover

Assortment of patterned fabrics

Pins

Needle

Embroidery floss

Small, sharp scissors

Buttons, beads, and trims (optional)

Pillow form

CREATE:

1. Use a fabric pencil to draw simple shapes directly on the pillow cover. Make sure the shapes aren't too small or intricate, and leave at least $1/2$ inch between each of them.

2. Back each shape with a piece of contrasting fabric pinned on the wrong side of the pillow cover with the pattern facing the fabric. The pinned fabric should be least 2 inches bigger than the shape it's backing all the way around.

3. Following the fabric pencil outline of the shape, sew the two layers of fabric together with a running stitch of brightly colored embroidery floss. A running stitch is a simple over-and-under stitch. You can decide how long or even the stitches should be.

4. With small, sharp scissors, cut out the solid-colored shape to reveal the patterned fabric below. Cut $1/8$ inch inside the running stitch.

5. Use your scissors to cut any excess fabric around each of your fabric shapes.

6. If you would like to sew on additional buttons, beads, or trim, now is the time. Trim can be sewn on by machine, if you like.

7. Slip your finished pillow cover onto the pillow form.

Left: Vintage plates add interest to a wall. Like little paintings, they can be hung in a cluster or arranged in a line that frames a doorway or window.

Right: I hand-painted the inset panels of this plain-Jane closet door and replaced the generic metal knob with an antique glass one.

Opposite: I went to town on the walls in this little guest bathroom, combining hand-painted roses with rubber-stamped leaves. I made the delicate curtains and floral valance in the window from vintage fabrics.

WALLS

Think of your walls as a backdrop. Whether clean and simple or richly patterned, they set the stage for family photographs, a beloved collection of vintage plates, or other treasures.

FAMILY ROOM

Just off the entryway and adjacent to the kitchen, our family room is exactly that—a space for our family. Bright and airy, it's a natural gathering place. Durable and unfussy, it accommodates the diverse requirements of a busy household—from three dogs and three kids to extended family and lots of friends. Everyone is welcome to relax and enjoy themselves here. Nothing is precious, and just about everything is washable!

This comfortable room, like all the rooms in our home, has evolved over time. As our kids have grown and our needs and tastes have changed, it too, has changed. Over the years, we've made simple changes to existing furniture pieces and walls, so much of what seems new is actually repurposed or embellished. These renovations—small, relatively quick, and inexpensive—in combination with new flea market finds and do-it-yourself projects, give this well-used space its fresh, charming character.

No matter where you live, your home should be an environment that feeds your senses and makes you feel content. If you love flowers, surround yourself with floral patterns. If you love color, accent your space with bold bursts of it. In our family room, I covered the drapes in hand-painted roses; used fun, handmade pillows (page 23) to spruce up a vintage daybed and classic slip-covered sofa; and lined a wall with a collection of colorful decoupage plates (page 37) I made myself. The possibilities are endless. And the rewards? Innumerable!

Hand-Painted Curtains or Lamp Shades

Curtains are conducive to hand-painting for many reasons: Paint can be used to cover a water stain, to add a splash of color that echoes or enhances a color scheme, or to bring a bit of interest to a plain or otherwise undistinguished curtain. Hand-painting a plain lamp shade is an easy and inexpensive way to solve the "generic" problem here as well: Buy a simple, one-color shade, and paint it in colors that complement your room.

GATHER:

Paper and pencil for sketching

Inspirational source materials

Plastic cups for mixing

Acrylic or latex paint

Golden brand GAC 900 fabric medium

Assortment of round and flat paintbrushes

Fabric swatch for testing

Curtain or lamp shade

Paper towels or rags

Container for water

DECORATIVE TRIM:

Fabric

Scissors

Measuring tape

Glue gun

CREATE:

1. Plan out your design on paper. Refer to inspirational source materials—such as wallpaper samples, fabric swatches, or vintage botanical illustrations—if you're having trouble thinking of ideas.

2. In the plastic cups, mix the colors you will need in quantities adequate to complete the project. Add GAC 900 to thin each one to the consistency of heavy cream.

3. Test the mixtures on a swatch of fabric that's the same color as or similar to the curtain or lamp shade. Adjust the consistency of the paint as necessary with GAC 900.

4. Begin painting your curtain or lamp shade.

5. To be safe, let the paint cure for at least 24 hours before using your hand-painted piece.

VARIATION: Add decorative trim to your lamp shade.

1. Once the paint has fully cured, cut two fabric strips or pieces of trim the length of the circumference of the lamp shade.

2. Use a glue gun to attach them to outside of the top and bottom edges of the shade.

COMFORT IS KEY

Make sure your family room has plenty of places to put up your feet, good light for reading, and coffee or side tables within arm's reach of every seat.

Glass Paperweight

I love glass paperweights. I display them grouped on a side table. They're also fun and easy to make. Find a small, clear glass bowl at a flea market or import shop, turn it upside down over some charms arranged on a piece of pretty wallpaper, and you have the makings of a one-of-a-kind paperweight.

GATHER:

Small (2 to 4 inches in diameter), clear glass bowl, cleaned and dried

Mat board

Pencil

X-ACTO knife

Mod Podge

Pretty wallpaper or other paper, photographs, or illustrations

Glue gun and glue sticks

Charms or other small objects

Decorative trim or tape

Felt

Scissors

CREATE:

1. Place the small glass bowl upside-down on a piece of mat board. With a pencil, lightly trace the rim of the bowl.

2. Use the X-ACTO knife to carefully cut out the traced circle. This will be the base of your paperweight.

3. Use Mod Podge to adhere the wallpaper, photograph, or illustration to the mat board. (All paper used for decoupage should be fairly lightweight, similar to computer paper.)

4. Use the glue gun to adhere charms or other small objects, such as beads, millinery flowers, or shells, to the base.

5. Use the glue gun to adhere the mat board base, decorated side up, to the rim of the bowl. Finish the edge with pretty fabric trim or tape.

6. Trace the rim of the paperweight on a piece of felt. Cut out the traced circle and use a glue gun to adhere it to the bottom of the paperweight.

Left: A simple bouquet of vintage crepe paper flowers is always a nice touch.

Right: Danny and I removed the wooden panels on this built-in armoire and replaced them with pieces of mirror and metal grate. Then I "distressed" the woodwork and added some flowers and vines. Voilà . . . from frumpy to fabulous!

Opposite: All of the seating in our family room, including this vintage daybed, is lined with soft, down-filled pillows and warm, comfy throws.

MIX AND MATCH

Don't be afraid to layer pattern on pattern. Remember that combining florals and geometrics is a good thing.

Decoupage Plates

Sometimes a large, empty wall is the elephant in the room. The space can be hard to fill, yet just as awkward to leave empty. I think a collection of similar objects, such as decoupaged plates, is the perfect solution. Clear glass plates are easy to find, and I use color copies of my own hand-painted designs as the artwork to back them.

GATHER:

Clear glass plate, cleaned and dried

Scissors

Paper cutouts, such as photocopies of family photographs, vintage wallpaper, or botanical illustrations (All paper used for decoupage should be fairly lightweight, similar to computer paper with matte finish)

Small foam brush

Mod Podge or diluted Elmer's Glue (3 parts glue to 1 part water)

Cork from a wine bottle

X-ACTO knife

Metallic gold marker

CREATE:

1. Plan the arrangement of paper cutouts on the plate. If using one large cutout, leave a $\frac{1}{2}$-inch border all the way around the outside edge.

2. Use the foam brush to spread thin coats of Mod Podge or diluted Elmer's Glue on the back of the plate. Do the same to the front of the paper cutouts (the side with the image).

3. Carefully place the paper cutouts, image side down, on the side of the plate coated in Mod Podge. Gently press the cutouts flat with your hands; work out any air bubbles or folds in the paper by rolling a cork over them, being careful not to tear the paper.

4. Let the plate dry to touch completely.

5. Use the foam brush to apply another coat of Mod Podge or glue to the back of the plate. Be careful not to lift the edges of the cutouts as you brush. Let the plate dry completely.

6. Repeat step 5 at least two more times, letting the plate dry completely between each application. I recommend 20 minutes between coats.

7. Use the X-ACTO knife to trim the edges of any cutouts extending beyond the rim of the plate.

8. Use the metallic gold marker to add a gold border around the edge of the plate.

EVERYDAY SPACES

KITCHEN AND
SUNROOM

KITCHEN

Our kitchen is both *functional and fun.* From the vintage crystal chandelier to the hand-painted cupboards, it's filled with things that make us happy—and so it should be, because we spend a lot of time in there! This well-used space is central to the hustle and bustle of family life. As conducive to conversation as it is to cooking, it reflects not only our taste, but also the graciousness and comfort that make our house a home.

Every kitchen has the basics: a sink, a stove, a counter, and a refrigerator. Beyond that, its design and contents can be as personal and eclectic as you choose. If you have treasured pieces you enjoy, don't be afraid to display them! Your kitchen, after all, should be a beautiful place where you love to be. With simple, inexpensive touches, it can suit the needs of you and your family and embody what you cherish most in life.

In our kitchen, we've managed to find spots for favorite flea market finds, such as the vintage mirror above the large sink. This mirror hung in my daughter's bedroom—until she decided she no longer wanted it there. I thought to myself, *I really like that mirror, where else could it go?* We moved it around,

tried it here and there, and finally, it ended up in the kitchen, where it's been ever since. Although the kitchen may seem an unlikely setting for an old mirror, it just works! The mirror reflects the sparkling chandelier above and the openness of the family room beyond. Best of all, it draws in light from outside—a pleasure for the person stuck doing the dishes.

I've done most of the decorative painting in our house myself, but I commissioned the cupboard doors because landscape painting isn't my forte. Inspired by English landscapes, I brought the interior panels, which pop out, to a local artist. She painted them in the pastoral style of the reproductions I gave her, emphasizing the aqua of the sky (my favorite color) and the many shades of green. This lovely, calm palette is a perfect backdrop for bursts of color—from simple fresh-cut flowers, a kitchen counter staple, to patterned dishware and linens.

The kitchen, like all the rooms in our house, is a work in progress. Year by year, we add new things, change old ones, and come up with new projects. In fact, I don't think it will ever be finished, and that's the fun of it!

Opposite: This sunny nook off the kitchen is a multipurpose space, perfect for daydreaming, doing homework, or both. I hand-painted the cabinets, drawers, and countertop to add interest to otherwise standard built-ins, and replaced generic knobs with vintage ones.

Right: We bought this sweet old stove many years ago from an antique shop. We knew we'd never use it as it was intended to be used, but we loved the tiles covering its surface and all the charming hardware and trim. Now, this unusual piece serves as a little coffee station in a corner of the kitchen, where we keep our coffee beans, grinder, and other supplies.

Next Page: Our kitchen is an offbeat mix. The antique crystal chandelier and mirror, the hand-painted cupboards, and the fresh-cut garden flowers are charming additions to this much-used space.

THINK OUTSIDE
THE BOX

Just because the kitchen
is a practical space doesn't mean
it can't be beautiful and inspiring.
Combine the functional
elements with more personal,
unexpected ones.

BREAD

SUNROOM

Our sunroom opens onto the terrace via French doors, connecting the inside of the house to the outside. It's a space we use every day—for family meals, casual lunches, and dinners with friends—it's full of favorite flea market finds and simple, handmade touches.

Part of the personality of any room comes from stories created and contained within it. The vines, which I painted up and down the walls, were based on a gift box design I created for a stationery company a long time ago. Years later, when the art director for the project came to lunch, she exclaimed, "Dena, I just realized, I'm sitting inside your box!" I had to laugh. Obviously, what I do during the day totally affects how I decorate our house!

I found the paintings of the lovely Japanese ladies above the piano at the flea market. When I spotted them, it was love at first sight. Shopping at the flea market is like that. You never know what you're going to find. When I'm drawn to a piece, I figure out how much I'm willing to pay for it before approaching the seller. If it turns out the price is higher than what I think is fair or can afford, I'll either politely try to talk the vendor down or walk away. In this case I decided to splurge but to spend no more than $500. When I asked the seller how much he wanted, he told me $60 for both. Now *that's* what treasure hunting is all about!

Our house is proof you can make a room beautiful, interesting, and entirely yours without spending enormous amounts of money. In fact, in seeking out less traditional places to buy things—such as consignment shops, tag sales, or flea markets—you'll discover a new world of possibilities. You'll find more for less, and the selection will always be fresh and different. When you do buy something—art or otherwise—make sure it's something you love, no matter what it's ultimately worth. We do go for that big splurge every now and then. But we rationalize expensive purchases because so much of what we use to decorate is handmade by us or was a flea market find. Place any new item somewhere, right away. If it creates the need to redecorate, so be it! That's half the fun!

In our house, we're not afraid of change, of adding or taking away, of painting or repainting. The elements in our home, like lively dinner guests, seem to demand conversation. In response, we move things around quite often. I love spaces that grow and change over time, for these are the rooms that give a home its personality—and its soul.

SIMPLE PLEASURES

Savor the scent of a garden rose, the sweetness of a fresh peach, or the everyday elegance of afternoon tea.

Paper Medallion

One rainy day my daughter, Lisa, and I made paper medallions, a fun project to do together. Once you've got the basic structure down, embellish to your heart's content! These pretty decorations can be made large or small and used to adorn anything from a wall to a gift box.

GATHER

Crepe or tissue paper in pretty colors

Scissors (and, if you have them, pinking shears)

Stapler (pliers-style staplers works best)

Glue gun and glue sticks

Other thin, decorative papers

Assortment of beads, buttons, millinery flowers, and trims

Ribbon

Cardboard backing

CREATE

1. Cut two 4-by-30-inch strips of tissue or crepe paper (if using crepe paper, the grain should run the short way). Using pinking shears, trim along one long side of each strip to give it a pinked edge. To create smaller and smaller circles, if desired, cut increasingly narrow pairs of strips and follow Steps 2 through 4.

2. Pleat one strip, making even folds across the short width. As you work, gather and hold the straight-edge side together with your index finger and thumb so the pinked edge fans out. The longer the original strip, the more ruffled the medallion will be.

3. Once you've created a full circle, stop folding, and trim any remaining paper.

4. Carefully staple the center of the medallion in place. Turn the medallion 45 degrees, and staple it again. If the circle still isn't secure, staple it one or two more times.

5. Repeat steps 2 through 4 with the rest of your strips.

6. Once you have several sets of smaller circles, layer them in order of size and glue them into a medallion. Embellish as you go with pretty bits of paper, beads, millinery flowers, or trim.

7. Glue several lengths of ribbon to the back of the medallion. To finish, cut a cardboard circle about 1.5 inch in diameter and affix it to the back of the medallion with glue.

Left: I covered this basic drum-shaped lampshade in a colorful paper, a simple and inexpensive way to customize generic lighting.

Right: Inspired by my antique dishes, I embellished this old cupboard, which I got at the flea market, with hand-painted flowers and patterns.

Opposite: With a quirky combination of flea market finds and handmade touches, our sunroom makes everyone feel at home.

SEATING

Things don't have to be traditional! Use one-of-a-kind chairs at the table—or even sofas. As long as it's comfortable, anything goes.

PROJECT

Hand-Painted Chair or Sofa

GATHER

Paper or fabric for sketching

Inspirational source materials

Acrylic or latex paint

Plastic cups for mixing paint colors

Golden brand GAC 900 fabric medium

Assortment of round and flat paintbrushes

Fabric swatch for testing paint colors

Furniture piece

Container for water

Paper towels

While this project is a bit more daunting than hand-painting a lampshade or curtain, the technique is the same. Perhaps start with one of those smaller projects before moving on to something as large as a sofa. Just know you can always slip-cover in the future if you want to change things up.

CREATE

1. Plan your design on paper or a piece of fabric similar in color to the one you'll be painting, referring to your inspirational materials as needed.

2. Mix your paints in the plastic cups. Use GAC 900 to thin each of your colors to the consistency of heavy cream.

3. Test the mixtures on a swatch of fabric that's the same or similar to the fabric you'll be painting. Adjust the consistency and colors as necessary.

4. Begin painting. Use the container of water to clean your brush between colors, and the paper towels for catching any drips.

5. Allow the paint to cure for at least 24 hours before using your hand-painted piece.

Left: I made these sweet and super-simple decorative glasses from vintage glassware, geraniums (freshly cut from my window boxes), and handmade paper fans.

Right: The whimsical vine-covered walls in our sunroom were inspired by the pattern for a gift box I designed many years ago.

Opposite: When it comes to table settings, I love to incorporate the unexpected, whether it's fresh-cut flowers in one-of-a-kind containers (don't be afraid to use something besides a traditional vase) or a collection of favorite finds.

SURROUND YOURSELF WITH BEAUTIFUL THINGS

Surround yourself with harmonious colors and objects that inspire you—from a favorite painting to fresh-cut flowers—and every room in your home will be a haven.

Opposite: A hand-painted vintage cupboard is the perfect place to display a favorite collection—in this case, everything from vintage salt-and-pepper shakers to ships in bottles.

Left: Fresh-cut garden flowers are among the simplest ways to add elegance to any room.

DECOUPAGE
Spruce up a lackluster
or worn surface with
decoupage.

Right: I decoup-
aged this piano
bench with pieces
of vintage wallpaper
and wrapping paper
that I'd collected
over the years.

Opposite: Vibrant
color is the order
of the day at this
cheerful table, set
for a brunch with
girlfriends.

PULL OUT
THE STOPS

Life is short! No matter what
the occasion, don't be afraid to use
your most cherished dishware,
silverware, and crystal. It will make
even the simplest gathering
feel special.

PLACES TO GATHER

DINING ROOM, LIVING ROOM, AND DEN

DINING ROOM

Our dining room is off the kitchen and family room, just past the *sunroom.* Once an extended porch, we enclosed it when we renovated. Although this room is elegant, it's nonetheless a comfortable space we use often—for family meals as well as for entertaining. The central feature is the dining table, an English pub table that we had widened by a skilled carpenter. The lovely Dutch chairs surrounding the table were a big splurge, but one that we treasure: They are hundreds of years old and each one is hand-painted with a different miniature landscape.

The dining room is the perfect place to display—and use—your favorite pieces, from silver and crystal to vintage linens and other family heirlooms. Pull out the things you love, no matter how precious or impractical, and enjoy them. Why not? Life is short, and doing so will make you and your guests feel special.

A combination of new and old, our dining room is a lively mix of purchases and homemade accents. A gold-framed rococo mirror—an over-the-top antiques store find— is set off by the hand-painted wall behind it. This vine-covered wall took some doing . . . and redoing. Originally, I envisioned a painted scene. I kept trying to create a mural but couldn't get it to work. Finally, I had an epiphany: Try something else! I painted the flowers first, then the yellow vine, and then the aqua ground. When the whole thing still didn't feel right, I took sandpaper to the flowers and softened them a bit. In the end, this pretty, floral pattern is a repeat of other decorative elements in the room—like the carved floral swag on the mirror, the flowery armature of the vintage chandelier, and the flower-patterned drapes—and thus is a more natural backdrop.

Don't hesitate to experiment or mix and match styles and patterns. In our dining room, pattern-on-pattern decorating gives the room its layered feel. The variety of lovely colors and shapes is visually pleasing, and the unexpected parallels bring harmony to the overall décor. The distinct personality of the room is found in the combinations, in the depth of detail, in the surprises and the delights. After all, what could be more wonderful than sitting in a beautiful room, surrounded by things you love, in the company of people you love?

PATTERN ON PATTERN

Setting complementary patterns against one another will add visual interest to your room and your table.

Velvet Rose Curtain Tieback

For elegant curtain tiebacks, I rolled and sewed strips of velvet into the shapes of roses and leaves.

GATHER:

Velvet

Scissors

Needle

Thread

Plain curtain tiebacks

Velvet leaves or other trim

CREATE:

1. Cut velvet into 4-by-24-inch strips. You'll need as many strips as you want roses.

2. Fold the strips in half lengthwise; the folded edge will form the top of the rose.

3. Shape the rose by rolling the strip. Roll tightly at first, tacking the layers into place with needle and thread as you go. As the rose takes shape, roll the velvet more loosely to allow it to "open" like the outer petals of a rose.

4. Sew the finished roses onto your curtain tiebacks. Sew on velvet leaves and other trim or millinery embellishments as needed.

Opposite: A view of the table and windows in our dining room, which was a porch until we enclosed it, from the living room.

Left: As is often the case with flea market finds, this vintage lamp came without its original shade. I knew I could look forever without finding the perfect something to complement the unusual stand. I solved the problem by hand-painting a simple stripe pattern and decorative trim on the top and bottom edges.

Covered Switch Plate

GATHER:

Scissors

Decorative paper, wallpaper, or lightweight fabric

Plastic switch plate

Double-sided permanent adhesive sheet

X-ACTO knife

Standard plastic switch plates are not only boring, they're unattractive—perfect targets for simple embellishment! They can be covered in vintage wallpaper, lightweight fabric, or decorative trims. Mix and match to create something pretty and eye-catching.

CREATE:

1. Cut pieces of wallpaper or fabric, $1/2$-inch longer than the width and length of the switch plate.

2. Cut a piece of double-sided adhesive sheet slightly larger than the switch plate. Snip off each of the four corners at an angle. Peel off the bottom protective layer and apply the sheet beneath to the front of the switch plate. Wrap the edges around the back of the switch plate.

3. Peel off the top protective layer. Adhere your paper, wallpaper, or fabric to the front of the switch plate, leaving a $1/4$-inch border on each side.

4. Fold the edges of the material around the plate.

5. Turn over the switch plate so that you are looking at the back, and with an X-ACTO knife, cut an X in the switch and screw openings.

6. Turn over the switch plate and fold the edges of the material through the switch openings to the back of the plate.

LIVING ROOM

Three steps down from the dining room, the living room is the largest and grandest space in the house. When we moved in, we thought for sure it would be the first room we'd renovate. As it turned out, it took us years to come up with a plan. We'd sit outside on the terrace and look in—or on the steps inside and look out. Eventually, we realized we wanted the room to really open to the outside to emphasize the relationship between the house and the garden. We replaced the large windows with a series of French doors. Now we can be inside and outside almost at the same time.

Decorating the room has been an ongoing project. Over the years, we've added pieces, moved them around, reupholstered or replaced them. Much of what we've done has been executed in beautiful fabrics. When I see a fabric I love, I buy it—even if I don't know what I'll do with it. If I have a favorite coat or dress I no longer wear, I save it. Down the road, I may use the fabric from it in another project—a pillow, a bolster, a chair back. As long as the material is sturdy and in good shape, I know I can find a way to make it into something new.

The stenciling on the walls is the newest addition to the living room. I designed and cut the template but hired someone else to do the actual painting, which required a tall ladder and a lot of measuring. A foil for the many floral patterns in this room, the stencil is more geometric and Moroccan in style. In the last decade, I've realized that my taste has begun to shift. I had always loved an eclectic look, especially the combination of a modern aesthetic mixed in with all of our antiques and flea market finds. But now I feel like we are leaning toward even bolder colors and geometric patterns mixed in combination with florals. The pairing of the two styles is somewhat unexpected and has given this room its distinct character.

Sometimes you'll be attracted to something different from anything else you have. You don't know why you like it or where you'd even put it. If it's affordable and you love it, bring it home! It may be that single, wonderful element that pulls together your room or project. When something inspires you, pay attention to it. More often than not, it's a glimpse of the future . . . and of what will make your home uniquely yours.

CHANGE IT UP

Find creative ways to use your more formal spaces. Move the furniture aside for a ballroom dancing party or a yoga class, or set up a small table and dine by firelight.

Fabric-Covered Chair Back

Sometimes an upholstered chair needs a patch or splash of something different to complement what's around it. For a fun and simple solution, "collage" the chair. This is the perfect opportunity to use that small piece of fabric you've always loved but haven't had a use for.

CREATE:

1. Carefully cut a piece of fabric the size and shape of the chair back, leaving an extra half inch of fabric all the way around.

2. Use a glue gun or Fabri-Tac to adhere the fabric to the chair. Start at one corner of the chair by adding glue to the folded-under raw edge and stick that to the corresponding corner of the chair. Work your way around the edge until the fabric is glued on all the way around.

3. Let the glue dry for one hour. Then, use a glue gun or Fabri-Tac to cover the rough edge where the fabric meets the chair with braid, ribbon, or decorative trim. Be sure to hide any messy glue spots and tuck in cut ends.

Fabric-Collage Pillow

My crafting closet is filled with fabric swatches I've collected over the years. As you can tell, I'm a fan of layering patterns and colors, and when I have a few different fabrics that work well together, I love to whip up "collaged" pillow covers.

CREATE:

1. Pin together pieces of fabric you love, no matter how small, to fit your pillow form.

2. Sew these little pieces together to make one large piece of fabric.

3. Follow standard sewing directions for making a zippered or button-on cover for a pillow form. These instructions can be found in pillow-making books or online.

Stenciled Wall

Stenciling a wall is a lot easier than you might think and is an inexpensive way to add interest to a room. If you're artistically inclined, you can design a pattern yourself, but if you're not, many lovely patterns already exist—online, in books, and in prepackaged kits. I've included one stencil at the back of the book.

GATHER:

Black permanent marker

Mylar sheet

X-ACTO knife

Ruler

Pencil

Level

Low-tack masking tape

Acrylic or stencil paint

Plate or palette

Airtight container

Rags or paper towels

Stencil brushes, either flat-tipped or domed

Damp sponge

CREATE:

1. With the permanent marker, draw or trace your stencil design onto a Mylar sheet.

2. Use an X-ACTO knife to carefully cut out the design.

3. Plot your pattern. With a ruler and pencil, lightly mark guidelines on the wall. Use a level to check all verticals and horizontals.

4. Beginning at the bottommost corner of the wall, adhere your stencil to the wall with low-tack masking tape.

5. Spread rags or paper towels on the floor to catch any spills or drips.

6. Put a small amount of acrylic or stencil paint onto a plate or palette. Store the remaining paint in an airtight container.

7. Dip the dry stencil brush into the paint and daub it on a rag or paper towel. You don't want excess or watery paint to run down the wall.

8. Holding the stencil brush perpendicular to the wall, apply the paint. For a speckled effect, lightly tap; for a smoother effect, use a circular motion.

9. Repeat steps 4 through 7 until the wall is covered.

10. If any paint accidentally drips or gets onto the wall, you can clean it up with a damp sponge before it dries. The wall will be dry in about 12 hours.

DEN

The den was once the dining room. This cozy, comfortable room is off the living room, linked visually but separated physically. Window boxes full of pink and fuchsia geraniums that flower year-round, thanks to our California weather, are visible through two picture windows, which open to the garden. Anchored in the corner by a slip-covered sectional sofa with lots of pretty pillows, the room's relaxed atmosphere makes it perfect for small gatherings of friends and family, children and dogs included.

Almost every surface is decorated—from the ceiling to the molding to the walls. I know, I know—I have a tendency to paint just about every flat surface in our house. I can't seem to help myself! The process really is a lot of fun, and once you've had some practice, the results speak for themselves. In the den, I began by painting the ceiling gold. When the paint I used didn't look quite right, Danny saved the day. With a piece of cheesecloth and some patience, he rubbed new paint over the old, creating a shimmery-gold matte luster in the process. This elegant ceiling casts a warm glow and makes the room feel inviting and intimate.

Sometimes, things perceived as decorating mistakes turn out to be fortuitous. In turning the "mistake" around, you may end up with something better than anything you could have imagined at the outset. We've painted the den three or four times in five years. We started with red, painted over it

with green, then cream with a pattern, which still didn't work and finally, we tried yellow with roses, and we love it. Still, the secret is to relax and to enjoy the adventure. I mean, what's the worst thing that can happen? If you don't like it, you'll just paint over it. No big deal!

The pretty antique mantel is another favorite "mistake." We saw it at the flea market, loved it, and thought it would be perfect for the family room. But when we brought it home, it was anything but. Too small for the space, it lacked presence and just didn't go with the personality of the room. At first, we didn't know what to do with it; finally, we moved it to the cozy den, where it fits perfectly.

There's an anecdote behind just about everything in this room. It's amazing how many aspects of our house are like that. We get things from the flea market or on trips—it's so nice to be on vacation and find something special to bring home with you, something that reminds you of a particular time or place. In repurposing or embellishing, the stories deepen, as does your personal connection to each room.

FAUX GILDING

Use a gold permanent marker to "gild" a white table, chair, or cabinet. Fill in carved-out sections, color in raised ones, or add a decorative border to make a plain piece more ornate and special.

Left: The colors of parrot tulips inspired the hand-painted molding in our den.

Right: I love to hand-paint molding. It's easy to do because it's naturally divided, and you can create a different simple pattern for each section. The decorative curtain rod below is standard rebar that I spray-painted gold.

FABRICS

Slip-cover furniture in washable fabrics. If you have children or pets, go with colors and textures that will hide wear and tear. White denim and canvas weather well, and when trouble strikes, a little bit of bleach works wonders.

Left: I transformed this sweet but worn bamboo side table with a swatch of fabric and some spray adhesive.

Right: This old-fashioned ceramic dish is perfect eye candy.

Opposite: I embellished this chandelier with antique crystal beads strung on wire.

CHANDELIERS

Chandeliers are like jewelry for the home. They will add elegance to any room—kitchens and bathrooms included.

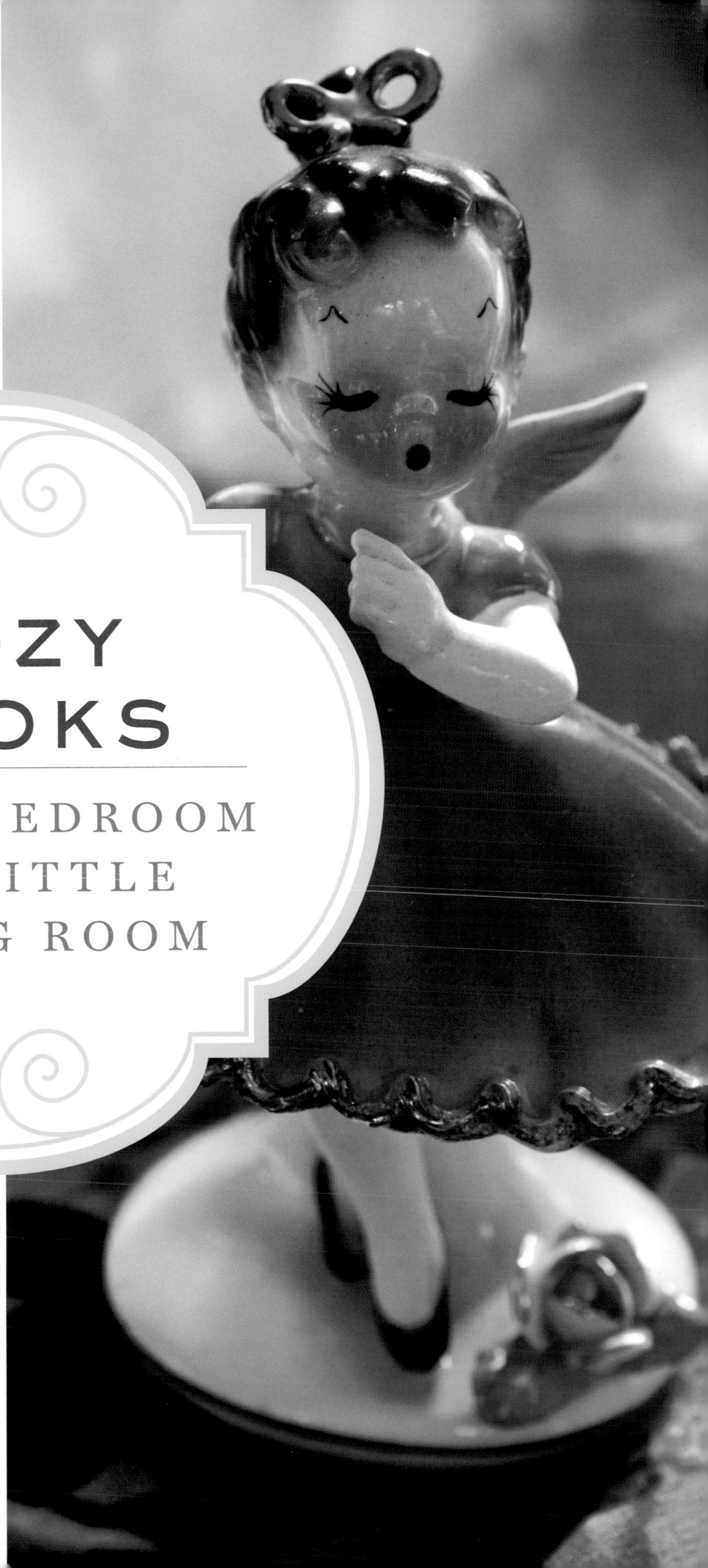

COZY NOOKS

LITTLE BEDROOM
AND LITTLE
SEWING ROOM

LITTLE BEDROOM

This tiny room off the family room originally housed our computer. As soon as we got laptops, we began to think about how else we could use the space. After deciding to make it a guest room, we moved in Lisa's old bed, which miraculously fit with only a quarter of an inch to spare! Since there's not a lot of extra space, every detail counts; it's important that each facet is thoughtfully executed and complementary to what's around it.

When considering a new piece of furniture for any room, be sure to examine the "bones" of that particular piece. Remember, you can't fix something that's fundamentally flawed in terms of structure or shape. If you're going to put time or money into repairing or decorating a piece, make sure that it will hold up in the long term and really work in your space—and that you love it.

A lot of us live with things we've outgrown, whether it's the style of a room or a particular piece of furniture. Part of what gives a house its vitality is its evolution. If your home grows and changes with you, if it reflects both where you are and where you've been, it will better suit where you're going. I'm amazed that we've been in our house for seventeen years, longer than we've been anywhere else. Over the years, as our needs have shifted, we've kept adding to and redecorating our basic space, which we still love. We're always finding new projects. We love change, and we love the process of making our house our own.

Stamped Pillow

Hand-stamping a pillow is a fun and rewarding project. Start with a store-bought basic pillow cover in a light color and a decorative stamp, and before you know it, you've created something beautiful and all your own—in colors that complement your décor.

GATHER:

Plastic cup for mixing

Acrylic paint

Golden brand GAC 900 fabric medium

Cardboard, cut to fit inside of your pillow cover

Pillow cover

Tape or tacks

Sheet of glass or Plexiglas

Brayer

Rubber stamp

Fabric for testing stamp

Container for water

Paper towels or rags

CREATE:

1. In a plastic cup, mix enough paint to execute your plan in full. Using GAC 900, thin the paint to the consistency of heavy cream.

2. Insert cardboard inside the pillow cover so the paint doesn't bleed through to the back of the fabric. Lay the cover on a flat surface and secure it with tape or tacks. Stamping will be easier and less messy if the fabric doesn't move and your work area is organized and clear of clutter.

3. Pour a little bit of paint onto a sheet of glass or Plexiglas. Roll it out with a brayer—a printmaking tool available at a local art supply or craft store—until you hear a snapping sound.

4. Apply paint to your rubber stamp with your brayer and do a series of test stamps on a similar piece of scrap fabric. Reroll your paint between tests. Adjust your technique and the consistency of the paint as needed.

5. Once you're pleased with the test results, begin work on your pillow cover! Use the container of water to clean your stamps between colors, and the paper towels for catching any drips. Allow the pillow cover to cure for 24 hours before placing it on a pillow.

VASES

Almost any container can be used for fresh-cut flowers. If the container you'd like to use won't hold water, line it with a smaller plastic container that will.

Opposite: When furnishing a small room, it's important to consider storage. This hand-painted vintage vanity has several drawers. Scented liners keep the contents smelling lovely.

Left: This is a detail of the romantic canopy that hangs at the head of the bed.

Right: In a small room, little goes unnoticed, including something as simple as an appliquéd curtain border.

LITTLE SEWING ROOM

This small room just "happened" when we enclosed the porch to make the dining room. All of a sudden, there was this sweet, small space we didn't know what to do with.

I began, as I often do, by painting, starting with the walls. Stripes are time-consuming because they have to be measured and taped out, but since this is a very small room I decided to go for it. Afterward, I added the vines and leaves, which were easier and quicker. You'll find that once you've had some success with decorative painting, you'll become more relaxed with the process and willing to experiment, which is when you can really go to town. Walls will lead to dishes, to picture frames, to fabrics, to furniture. The possibilities open up and will come to you more naturally as you gain experience and confidence.

Next, I framed the doorway with a fabric curtain, which made the entrance softer and more inviting. If you like the idea of an arch or a scalloped doorway but you can't afford or don't want to renovate, you can make the change with either a curtain or a valence.

One step leads to another; one project jump-starts the next. As you work, you'll find yourself inspired. New ideas will come to mind. The fun of a small room is that one tiny change can transform the space—a few new pillows, a reupholstered chair, a decoupaged table, a hand-painted frame. If a room has just two lamps but you make two fabulous lamp shades for them, you can alter the feeling of your space in an afternoon—quickly and at little cost!

GLASS TABLETOPS

Transform a not-so-interesting tabletop with a display of antique linens, fabric, paper, vintage cards, family photographs, or other flat mementos arranged beneath a layer of glass, where they'll be visible but protected.

One-of-a-Kind Slipcover

GATHER:

Plain slipcover

Coordinating fabrics

Scissors

Pins

Sewing needle

Embroidery floss

Sewing machine (optional)

Slipcovers are a great way to revamp a chair or sofa without the cost and time of reupholstering or buying new. Changing the look of even just one chair in a room can have a big impact on the whole space. I like to have white slipcovers on hand for my chairs because they're versatile and I can easily add to them. If you are unable to sew your own solid slipcovers, you can hire someone else to do it or see if there's one for sale that fits on your furniture. I sewed the shapes on by hand using brightly colored embroidery floss. Now if I ever want to change my slipcover design, I can easily cut the thread, pull the shapes off, and start over with a new idea!

CREATE:

1. Tie your slipcover to your chair or sofa

2. Cut circles, leaves, or other shapes in different sizes out of your coordinating fabrics.

3. Pin the fabric shapes onto your slipcover, rearranging them until your layout is to your liking.

4. Untie the slipcover with pinned shapes and take it off the furniture.

5. Using a needle and thread or a sewing machine, sew $1/4$ inch in from the outer edges of your fabric shapes. If you're sewing by hand, use a simple over-and-under running stitch. The edges may fray a little—this adds to the charm and one-of-a-kind look of your slipcover.

PRIVATE HAVENS

MASTER BEDROOM SUITE

SITTING ROOM

This lovely room was the master bedroom until we built an addition many years ago. The newest feature of the space is the hand-painted wall, which was inspired by a vintage wallpaper pattern I saw in a magazine. I wanted to re-create the pattern's overall feel and subject matter (vines and leaves, birds, and flowers) in a softer palette and more lyrical style. My finished painting is reminiscent of the old pattern but fresh and personal. I'm happy with the calmer colors—in particular, the aquas and greens, which are echoed throughout the room.

Inspiration for projects can come from anywhere—a piece of vintage wallpaper, a swatch of fabric, a flower in your garden. As time goes on, recognizing and gathering source material becomes second nature. In the meantime, when you see something you like, remind yourself to save it! I have a series of files where I store images and items that inspire me. You never know when or in what context that specific element may become useful. A spirit of adventure—and some research— goes a long way toward turning an idea into reality.

I've been known to paint just about anything: Virtually nothing is untouchable in my book (unless it's already been decorated by someone else). If painting works, great! And if it doesn't, there's still time for Plan B. For instance, I hand-painted these matching leather chairs, but figured I could reupholster if the painting didn't turn out right. I bought them for next to nothing at the flea market and had little to lose. I combined acrylic paint with GAC 900, a fabric painting medium, and dove headfirst into the project. Happily, the paint is permanently adhered, and I successfully transformed two chairs from drab to delightful!

Small projects such as these are inexpensive yet gratifying on many levels. With a few supplies and a little time, you can turn something run-of-the-mill into a unique and personally relevant piece. You can both enliven a room and make it yours, a process that brings deep and lasting satisfaction. When your home is filled with beautiful things that you love and have gathered—or made yourself—it affirms who you are, what your aesthetic is, and how you choose to live your life.

PILLOWS

Plenty of pillows soften a sofa or chair, provide accent colors, and are easily changed with the seasons. Re-cover your pillows, and you'll update the look of your room in no time flat.

Painted Wall

When it comes to painting your walls, don't be afraid to try something new—or to work step by step. Part of the charm of a hand-painted wall is that it's not perfect, not "store-bought." If you make a mistake you can't live with, you can always paint over it!

GATHER:

Latex paint for base color

Pencil

Inspirational source materials

Acrylic paint for decorative elements

Plastic cups for mixing

Paper for testing colors

Cotton rags or paper towels

Assortment of round and flat paintbrushes

Container for water

Damp sponge

CREATE:

1. If you are planning on changing the base color of your wall, now is the time to paint it with the latex paint. Otherwise, move on to Step 2.

2. Lightly pencil vines and leaves on the wall, freehand, referencing the materials you've collected as needed.

3. Mix your colors. Use a separate disposable mixing cup for each of the colors you will use for your wall art. I like to test colors on a piece of paper before I begin painting to be sure they complement each other.

4. Spread rags or paper towels on the floor to catch any spills or drips.

5. Begin painting the vines and leaves you outlined in Step 2. Use the water container to clean your brush between colors or to thin out your acrylic paint. Thinning your paint with a little water will make it smoother and decrease the opacity. To erase any acrylic paint on your wall before it has dried, just wipe a damp sponge over it. Allow the wall to dry for 24 hours.

Left: At the flea market, I often come upon a beautiful piece of embroidery or needle-point that I can't live without. If it's too delicate to make into a pillow, I frame it and hang it on the wall.

Right: If I could, I would live in my garden, which is why I put fresh-cut flowers in every room of my house.

Opposite: The mirror in this favorite corner of my sitting room is actually the door to a built-in bookcase.

FIREPLACE
A working fireplace is wonderful for cooler weather or a romantic evening at home. Keep logs on hand just in case!

CLOSET

There are no two ways about it: A well-organized closet is an anchor. It fosters a sense of peace and well-being. And if it's beautiful as well, it will be a source of great pleasure and inspiration. It's easy to overlook your closets when redoing your home, yet closet makeovers are among the most satisfying of projects. And frankly, there's no better therapy!

My friend Ingrid performed the miraculous transformation of what was probably the dullest room in my house: the clothes closet off my bedroom. Her secret weapon? Liquid starch, which she used to adhere fabrics to the walls, drawers, and shelves. Unlike traditional wallpaper, fabric can be peeled off, washed, and even reused—amazingly enough, without leaving any residue on the wall.

Though few people see my closet, let alone spend any time in it, the simple pleasure it brings to me day in and day out is hard to top. In the mornings, I can see my options clearly: Everything is there, carefully hung or folded, and it's displayed in practical yet charming ways. At the end of the day, there's a place for everything and everything's in its place—something not to be underestimated in the face of an often way-too-busy schedule.

INSIDE AND OUT

Wallpaper or paint the inside of your closet in a lovely pattern or color and line or paint the insides of your drawers and cupboards.

Fabric-Covered Wallpaper

The perfect solution for a dorm room or a rental apartment, covering a wall in fabric is easy to do—and when the time comes, easy to undo.

GATHER:

Soap and water

Tape measure

Scissors

Lightweight fabric

Liquid fabric starch

Bucket

3-inch short-bristled paint brush

Tacks or pushpins

X-ACTO knife

CREATE:

1. Use soap and water to wash the wall you plan to cover.

2. Measure the wall, adding 1 inch to the top and bottom. Cut the fabric to fit. If the fabric is patterned and more than one piece is required to fill the space, be sure to line up the motifs.

3. Pour the liquid starch into a bucket.

4. Use the paint brush to apply starch to the top half of the wall. Smooth the fabric into position from the top down, leaving 1 inch along the top edge to be trimmed later. Hold the fabric in place with tacks or pushpins while you apply the bottom half.

5. Using the paint brush, apply starch to the bottom half of the wall. Smooth the remaining fabric into position, leaving 1 inch at the bottom to be trimmed later.

6. Apply starch to the fabric from the top down with your sponge, removing bubbles and wrinkles as you go. Be sure the fabric is absorbing the starch evenly.

7. Repeat steps 4 through 6 for each additional piece of fabric.

8. When fabric is completely dry (about 4 hours), use an X-ACTO knife to carefully trim the overhanging fabric at the top and bottom edges. wait 24 hours before putting clothes back into the closet.

BATHROOM

My sister-in-law, Amy, a former faux-finisher, painted the ceiling in our master bathroom a sky blue filled with soft white clouds. The tub below is set between a window overlooking the garden and a series of three painted panels—pretty, light-filled landscapes inspired by French Impressionist paintings—which I painted myself while lying on the bathroom floor (I don't recommend this as a good painting position!).

The greens, golds, and blues of the paintings surrounding the wooden tub and the ceiling are echoed throughout the room. Gold filigree, which I hand-drew with a fine-tip marker on the drawers and cupboard doors, lend interest to otherwise plain cabinetry—as do the vintage-style glass knobs.

Your bathroom can and should be as inviting and comfortable as any other room in your house. With simple touches and considerate details, this practical space can also be a beautiful one.

PRACTICAL YET PRETTY

Be matter-of-fact when it comes to the basics, then have fun with the details: paint the walls and ceilings a beautiful color; store sundries in eye-catching containers; and don't forget the fresh-cut flowers

Above: This little box was a flea market find and I love having shells throughout the house just because they're beautiful.

Left: The drawers and cupboards in the master bathroom, though fundamentally nothing special, were easy to transform. I used a gold permanent marker to "gild" the fronts and then replaced the generic knobs with vintage-looking glass ones.

Necklace Peg Board

GATHER:

Ribbons, trim, paper, fabric, yarn

Scissors

Wooden peg board

Glue gun

Mod podge and foam brush

Chenille yarn for trim

Vintage buttons

Coming up with interesting ways to store your costume jewelry can be a challenge. My ever-growing collection of vintage necklaces is a case in point. If kept in a box or a drawer, it inevitably becomes a tangled mess. I wanted it to be organized and accessible, as well as visible and visually pleasing. A simple peg board embellished with a vintage wallpaper border, trim, and vintage buttons was a perfect quick-and-easy solution.

CREATE:

1. Cut strips of ribbon, trim, patterned paper, fabric, and/or yarn the length of your wooden peg board.

2. Use the mod podge and foam brush to adhere any paper you are using. Use a glue gun to adhere the strips to the front of the board and chenille yarn to the board's edges. See page 37 for the technique.

3. Use the glue gun to attach buttons to the fronts of the wooden pegs.

4. Let the peg board cure for 24 hours before hanging.

CANOPY

A bed canopy instantly adds a romantic, princess-y feel to any bedroom.

BEDROOM

Our *bedroom is our sanctuary.* Visually and physically soothing, it's a place to which we retreat, a space in which we're surrounded by things we both love—things we've collected together over time. It's romantic and peaceful, uncomplicated and comfortable. Here, the shift from dreams to reality occurs every morning. From this spot, we are restored and reconnected to who we are as individuals and as a couple.

Our bedroom opens into the garden outside, and we greet the day from our wrought-iron four-poster bed. This ritual inevitably begins with two cups of coffee—and at least one barking dog.

Every bedroom should contain a bit of fantasy. In ours we found the perfect piece in a work of art. For years, I'd imagined a picture, an old oil painting of palm trees on an exotic beach, maybe a French island in the Caribbean. I'd go to the flea market with this image in the back of my mind. After years of searching for it, I saw just the painting one Saturday as I walked down an aisle in the Sausalito flea market with a friend. I hurried toward the picture, but the moment I got to the booth, a man reached for it. I thought to myself, *That's* my *painting—you've no idea!* (The rule of the flea market is that when someone picks up an item, it's his until he puts it down.) Not wanting to appear overeager, I held back.

As the man looked at the piece, I hovered, waiting for him to set it aside, which—of course—he didn't. As he pulled out a loupe and slowly examined the surface, I groaned. At this point, my friend insisted we walk away; we planted ourselves in a booth selling bicycles across the way, from which we could watch the scene unfold. Over the next half hour, the man put the piece down only to pick it up again quickly. Then, when he really put it down, my friend pushed me toward it. I tripped over the bikes, landed on the ground, and when I looked up, he was holding the painting again! Finally, he put it down for more than ten seconds, at which point, I jumped up again, asked the vendor for the price, paid in cash, and fled! I don't think the guy knew what hit him!

A bedroom houses our stories as much as ourselves—our memories of the past and our hopes for the future. It's host to the full range of human emotion, from the mundane to the most profound; it's where passion should be as welcome as sleep.

Left and opposite: A colorful tassel is a striking detail on this hand-painted armoire. A flea market find, this wonderful piece of furniture, which holds (and hides) our TV set, has good, solid bones but was nothing special—until I pulled out the paints and brushes.

Right: A good bedside table is essential. Though I hand-painted this particular piece, which sits to the right of my bed, decoupage would be gorgeous, too.

REPURPOSE

Hide your entertainment and audio systems. Redo the inside of a favorite piece of furniture to make it suit another purpose.

PASTELS

A pastel palette is soothing and will complement a range of colors and styles in bedding, curtains, and other fabrics.

Left: I dressed up a plain table with a skirt made out of a curtain (a vintage tablecloth or other fabric would also work).

A ROOM OF ONE'S OWN

HALLWAY AND UPSTAIRS BEDROOMS

HALLWAY

Our upstairs hallway extends to the back of the house, and four bedrooms branch off it: Lisa's room, which used to be our eldest daughter Rachel's room; a guest room, which used to be our son David's room; Lisa's old bedroom, which we now use mainly for storage and projects and are converting into a gym; and our master bedroom. Now that two of our three children have grown up and left the nest, it's been fun to reconsider each of these spaces, their function, and their design.

The hallway is painted aqua, a color echoed in each of the rooms, with a simple, hand-painted vine pattern on top. To add visual interest to what was a fairly mundane part of the house, we replaced plain doorknobs with vintage glass ones, and generic light fixtures with antique chandeliers and sconces. Simple yet thoughtful touches such as these give this well-traveled path a light, airy character and connect it aesthetically to the rooms beyond.

Opposite and left: I hand-painted the wall and small dresser in what used to be Lisa's room. Now that Rachel's left the nest and Lisa's moved into Rachel's old room, we plan to convert this space into a gym.

Above: I gave this hallway sconce a makeover using wire and beads—simple to do, and the results are fabulous.

LIGHTING
Replace or embellish generic light fixtures.

LISA'S BEDROOM

A *home is a collaboration in which each member of the household brings something to the table.* Just as each family member has a distinct personality, each has individual interests and needs. When it comes to the design and decoration of children's rooms, in particular, it's important to remember this. A child's room is his or her own personal haven and should be decorated accordingly.

Our youngest daughter, Lisa, adores flowers, and her room has always been filled with them. She loves to make and embellish things— like mother, like daughter. Over the years, we've worked together and separately on each and every element in her room—from the hand-painted walls and wallpapered ceiling to the many pretty things decorating the space. Though rarely neat and tidy, this joyful room reflects its spirited inhabitant—definitely one of the most stylish teenagers I know.

As children grow up, their interests and needs evolve—as do their rooms. What will work for a five-year-old girl will not be suitable for one at thirteen—from a practical standpoint or an aesthetic one. If you're purchasing new furniture, think beyond the present: The future is just around the corner. And in terms of the design, stay flexible! When your child is ready for a change, enjoy the process of making it together.

Right: Using some fabric adhered with liquid starch, my friend Ingrid worked magic on the glass sconce shades in Lisa's bathroom.

CHILDREN'S ROOMS

Encourage your children to help choose the color and décor of their personal spaces.

Left and right: An assortment of pillows in festive colors and patterns.

Opposite: Ingrid used liquid starch to adhere fabric to the glass-paneled doors of Lisa's medicine cabinet. Super sweet!

GUEST ROOM

Believe it or not, this pretty guest room once belonged to our son, and it had dark blue walls and wood paneling. We decided to redo it recently, after David graduated from college and moved out. Since then, the space has been transformed and most of its contents updated or replaced.

Sometimes one change will launch a thousand more. In the case of David's room, it was painting the closet doors, which were the plainest, most generic doors ever. They had boring, basic knobs, no decorative or architectural features, no personality whatsoever. By adding molding, we gave visual interest in the form of "panels," on which my daughter Rachel and I hand-painted flowers. Once the closet doors were made over, the overall feeling of the room was, too. We had a direction and could move forward with the rest of the room.

Guest rooms are in-between rooms. They should be complete in and of themselves, yet in terms of their design and decoration, be open enough to allow visitors to make the space theirs while in residence. There should be room in the closet, empty drawers, and a place to set a suitcase or duffel bag. Remember, if the space is cluttered with too many of your personal items, it won't be nearly as welcoming or relaxing.

Left: I adhered buttons to the hooks of these traditional curtain holders.

Right: I used two favorite mix-and-match pieces of vintage needlepoint, both flea market finds, to upholster this otherwise nondescript chair in our guest room.

Opposite: Our guest room is beautifully decorated but not cluttered, so guests have the space they need to unpack and make themselves at home.

TRIAL RUN

Test out your guest room.
Spend the night there yourself
to make sure it's comfortable
and contains everything a
houseguest would need
or want.

Your guest will appreciate being able to unpack fully. Make sure there's room in the dresser drawers and closet, along with an adequate supply of hangers.

Opposite: Fresh-cut flowers and a ceramic box adorn a decoupaged tabletop.

Left: Transforming something as basic as closet doors will shift the character of a room. Here, I created "panels" with molding and a bit of decorative painting—quick and easy, but the results are fantastic.

FRAMES

Gather a selection of frames and paint them all the same color to create a unified but interesting wall display.

TOILETRIES

Provide plenty of fresh towels and other amenities, such as shampoo, soap, and toothpaste, in the guest bathroom.

Above: In the guest bathroom, sundries are stored in elegant containers.

Opposite: I used liquid starch and fabric to embellish these basic sconces.

INSPIRING SPACES

STUDIO AND GARDEN

STUDIO

Each of us needs a space in which to be creative, a space to sew a pillow or write a poem. It doesn't have to be big, but it has to be comfortable, and it must be yours to organize and use as you see fit. It can be as simple as a corner with an old kitchen table, a chair, and a good light, or as over the top as you can imagine. What's most important is that it's there and that it suits you. Your work space should reflect your personality and style—as opposed to anyone else's. It should be a place in which you can be yourself and where you feel completely comfortable.

My studio overlooks our garden, which is a constant source of pleasure and inspiration to me. I sit on a high drafting stool that Danny gave me—he had it upholstered in soft velvet and trimmed with a velvety leopard print as a birthday present. I happily perch on this special seat, surrounded by things I love: beautiful swatches of fabric, old tin containers filled with buttons, millinery flowers, and tiny bits of vintage this-and-that stored in glass-topped watchmaker's tins. Projects in various stages of completion and the materials necessary to execute them are everywhere: tubes of paint, paintbrushes, paper, and more.

There's little separation between my work as a textile and product designer and my life. I spend most days in my studio, which is physically connected to the house so that I can be at home and at work simultaneously. For me, the distinction between the two is blurry. As much as my job is an ongoing project, so is the house. Both are always changing; both are works in progress. They continually inspire one another, and the connection between them, the constancy of that, is what centers me.

Left: I want my workspace to be as
comfortable and lovely as any other
space. Here, a vintage rug cozies up the
wooden floor.

Right and opposite: I love to find fun and
interesting ways to store my materials.

Opposite: A colorful view of my new workspace and "showroom." Bolts of my fabric line the shelves in the background.

Left: This pillow-covered daybed in my studio is perfect for catnaps.

GARDEN

Our garden offers endless surprise and delight: *the periwinkle blue of a delphinium, a ripe peach, a sparrow splashing in a birdbath.* It's an extension of our home, and the two are inextricably linked. The house opens up to the garden on all sides, and the garden spills into the house, in the form of floral-inspired patterns and colors. Window boxes full of geraniums mark the transition.

Flowers and design, each in their own way, inform each other, literally and poetically. Not unlike a garden, a home is always in flux.

New projects blossom to replace the old. One idea inspires the next. Things are moved and combined in unexpected ways. There's an underlying structure to the inevitable evolution of things, a palpable life beat.

Like an enchanting house, a beautiful garden invites meandering. Ours is a series of interconnected "rooms," each one enclosed by something old—a wrought-iron fence, an antique arbor, a stone wall. A walk along the path that wends its way in and out never yields the same experience twice. In a garden, as in art and life, there will always be new things to discover.

INSPIRATION

Be open to inspiration
wherever you are. Who knows?
You may find the colors for
your kitchen wall in a friend's
garden, or somewhere
less expected.

SEATING

Place comfortable chairs where the view of your garden is loveliest.

Above: Three Adirondack chairs invite conversation in an elevated section of the rose garden.

Opposite: This vintage birdhouse was a flea market find.

Opposite: The wooden bridge and path-way that lead up to Seven Oaks Ranch.

Above: I love to greet the day with a stroll through my garden and a pair of scissors.

SURPRISE AND DELIGHT

Make your garden an
endless source of pleasure,
a lovely mix of nature's
offerings and your own
hard work.

Above: The lupines in my garden seem to reach for the sun.

Left: A view up the stairs to one of our favorite places in the whole world.

ENTERTAINING

ENTERTAINING

Danny and I love to entertain, and when we do, we want to be sure that our friends and family feel comfortable in our home. It's all about making your guests feel special and cared for. To that end, nothing we own is so precious that we're ever nervous about using it. All of our communal spaces are meant to be lived in, and their contents are meant to be enjoyed. We not only want our guests to feel welcome, we want them to relax and have fun.

No matter how impromptu or casual the get-together, when you invite people into your home, you want the experience to be special. You want guests to feel you've done something a little out of the ordinary in honor of their visit. The "extras" need not be fancy or expensive. Rather, it's the simple embellishments and the setting that make an event—no matter its size—gracious and memorable.

A shared meal is the highlight of many gatherings, with the whole table as a centerpiece. It can reflect the theme—if there is one—and establish the overall tone of the event. Though a table set for a birthday party will be different from a table set for Thanksgiving dinner, both should be thoughtfully composed. A wonderful centerpiece, homemade place cards, beautiful table linens, and unexpected eye candy will serve to make the experience more magical.

Entertaining is a form of sharing who you are and what you love. It reveals your personality and unique way of doing things. In being true to yourself, you'll create an atmosphere that's natural and comfortable to others. Though the experience to be had is a gift from you to your guests, it should be a source of pleasure to you both. Remember: If you're having fun, chances are good that your guests are, too!

SET THE STAGE

A colorful tablecloth sets the stage for a beautiful table and unifies its components. Use a sewing machine to stitch together strips of fabric you love into a desired shape and size. A repeated stripe of the same fabric, which can be ruched for added charm, will tie diverse elements together.

Layered Glass Vases

A pretty flower arrangement is a welcome addition to just about any surface—table or otherwise. Create a collection of vases to coordinate with your dishware, flowers, setting, or occasion.

GATHER:

Cylindrical glass vases in two sizes: one that fits into the other

Color Xeroxes of fabric, wallpaper, gift wrap, or other patterned materials

Double-stick tape

CREATE:

1. Cut the color Xeroxes to line the larger of the two vases.

2. Use double-stick tape to adhere the paper to the inside of the vase.

3. Insert the smaller vase into the larger one and fill it with water and fresh-cut flowers.

DECORATIONS

For a garden party, decorate the trees, fence, or other nearby structures with banners, streamers, or vintage lanterns filled with flowers.

Left and right: I created these floral
decorations for my daughter Lisa's
birthday party.

Opposite: An ethereal tulle tablecloth skirt
with green sheet moss and loads of flowers
set the perfect stage for Lisa's party.

Teacup Party Favors

Embellish your table with delightful teacup party favors, which double as place-card holders. These sweet souvenirs are fun to make and even more fun to give away. Pick up mismatched teacups and saucers at thrift stores, tag sales, and flea markets. Floral supplies are inexpensive and can be purchased at a local flower shop or craft store.

GATHER:

Knife

Floral foam brick that's been soaked in water

Variety of teacups and saucers

Water tubes for fresh-cut flowers

Small, fresh-cut flowers

Green moss

Black permanent marker

Decorative paper

Toothpicks

Tiny clothespins

Tape

Miniatures, such as dollhouse furniture, tiny flowerpots, and paper parasols

Glue gun and glue stick

CREATE:

1. Use a knife to cut a piece of dampened floral foam to fit into a teacup, leaving a 1-inch space at the top.

2. Fill a plastic water tube with water, poke a small nosegay of fresh-cut flowers through the hole at the top, and insert the tube into the floral foam.

3. Cover the floral foam (and edge of the water tube) with moistened green moss.

4. Use black permanent marker to write your guest's name on a piece of decorative paper cut into a small banner shape. Attach the banner to a toothpick with miniature clothespins and tape, if needed. Insert the place card into the floral foam.

5. Complete your vignette with miniatures placed on top. These can be hot glued to the moss if you don't want them to come off. Use your imagination, and have fun!

FUN AND FABULOUS

Unexpected splashes of mixed and matched color and pattern will delight the eye and create a festive table.

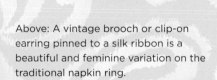

Above: A vintage brooch or clip-on earring pinned to a silk ribbon is a beautiful and feminine variation on the traditional napkin ring.

Opposite: Layers of beautiful, harmonious color and pattern, in combination with flowers (of course!) and my prettiest dishes, give this table setting its charming character.

Left: Party drinks are fun to decorate. Paper parasols are among my favorites; for something more custom, hot-glue ribbon, fabric flowers, or other trinkets onto their tops.

Right: Chinese lanterns hang from the "ceiling" of a tent installed in my garden for a summertime pool party.

Opposite: For this party seating, I used safety pins to temporarily cover a few pillows in fun fabric that coordinates with the poolside setting.

Fabric Banner

I like to be in a happy environment—especially when I'm entertaining! Hanging a fabric banner from the trees automatically makes the tone of the space more fun and cheerful. This project can become more or less permanent (and complicated) by hemming each of the triangles or using paper in place of fabric.

GATHER:

Ruler

Pencil

Paper

Scissors

Pins

Assortment of fabrics

Pinking shears

Fabri-Tac

Decorative trim

Ribbon

Pins

Iron-on adhesive (optional)

Iron (optional)

Tacks

CREATE:

1. Use a ruler, pencil, paper, and scissors to make a triangle pattern that is 9 inches tall and 6 inches across.

2. Pin the pattern to the fabric, and cut the fabric with pinking shears. Repeat until you have enough triangles to make a banner.

3. Use Fabri-Tac to adhere decorative trim to the triangle fronts.

4. Cut a piece of ribbon the desired length of the banner.

5. Pin triangles back-to-back along both sides of the ribbon, leaving 10 inches at either end.

6. Use Fabri-Tac or iron-on adhesive to adhere the triangles to the ribbon.

7. Tack your banner at each end of the ribbon to hang it.

Candy Cake

Sweeten your table with a yummy candy cake! It's not only fun to create, it makes a festive centerpiece that guests of all ages will love. For a final touch, embellish the cake stand with fringe or other decorative trim.

GATHER:

Styrofoam cake dummies

Cake stand

White frosting, either homemade or store-bought

Assortment of candy with interesting and/or colorful wrappers

Double-sided tape

Decorative trim

CREATE:

1. Use frosting to adhere a Styrofoam cake dummy to your cake stand.

2. Add additional dummies to create a tiered "cake" of the desired height and size. Use frosting to adhere the layers to each other.

3. Use the frosting to adhere each piece of wrapped candy to your Styrofoam cake. Trim the exposed edges with a frosting border.

4. Edge the rim of the cake stand with double-sided tape and cover with decorative trim.

Left: Vintage bottles and other nontraditional containers can make wonderful vases.

Right: Here, I sandwiched fabric between two glass plates.

Opposite: A table set by the fireplace in the living room is the perfect setting for an elegant dinner with friends.

EPILOGUE

I *remember when Danny and I bought our first house, which we named our "Flintstone House."* We were in our twenties, and the only reason we could afford what we decided looked like a giant mushroom (it really did!) was because it had been on the market forever. Literally, no one else wanted it. As soon as we moved in, we began to redecorate. I had this crazy idea to paint the living room pink—a soft, pale, beautiful pink. We eagerly purchased supplies and worked late into the night. When we awoke the next morning, however, we discovered that the lovely color we'd chosen was, in fact, anything but. In the light of day, being in our new living room was like being inside a giant pink bubblegum bubble. Horrible! We were briefly dismayed and then came up with a plan B. We headed back to the paint store and this time settled on an off-white. Three coats later, the pink was but a story we still laugh about every time we set out to repaint a room!

Life stories are part of what make a house a home. They're often triggered by a particular event or object. They connect us to one another, over time and space. They're what give our surroundings depth, personality, and meaning. A home offers a foundation from which to grow—as a person and as a family. As much as it provides stability, it offers opportunity for change. Sometimes I can't believe we've lived in our current house for almost eighteen years. So much has happened along the way, including raising three children, quite a few dogs, and lots of other small animals. In reorganizing, repainting, and redecorating to accommodate the changes, we've always strived to keep our familiar surroundings fresh and suited to the needs of our family at the time. The many fun projects—of all sizes—have been the icing on the cake.

I hope this book inspires you to think of your own home as a work-in-progress: to hand-paint your walls, to embellish a pillow or lamp shade, or to repurpose a piece of furniture. I hope it inspires a sense of adventure and a do-it-yourself spirit, because you can do it! If you have an idea, go with it! If it works, hooray! And if it doesn't? Well, don't be afraid to try something else. Either way you cut it, you'll have gained something in the process . . . and a good story or two.

DENA'S FAVORITE ARTISANS AND SHOPPING SPOTS

FAVORITE FLEA MARKETS:

Alameda Point Antiques Faire

First Sunday of every month

2900 Navy Way (at Main Street)
Alameda, CA 94501

www.alamedapointantiquesfaire.com

Paris Flea Market at Porte de Clignancourt

Officially called Le Marché aux Puces de Paris/Saint-Ouen, also known to Parisians as Les Puces (The Fleas). This is the largest antique market in the world! It covers seven hectares (17.3 acres) and receives 150,000 visitors each weekend.
www.marcheauxpuces-saintouen.com

Rose Bowl Flea Market

Second Sunday of every month

1001 Rose Bowl Drive
Pasadena, CA 91103

www.rgcshows.com

FAVORITE STORES:

ABC Carpet & Home

Ten floors offering an inspired collection of rugs, furniture, antiques, home textiles, accessories, and sustainable furnishings. See site for other locations.

888 & 881 Broadway
New York, NY 10003
(212) 473-3000

www.abchome.com

Big Daddy's Antiques

Los Angeles Warehouse
3334 S. La Cienega Place
Los Angeles, CA 90016
(310) 769-6600

San Francisco Warehouse
1550 17th Street
San Francisco, CA 94107
(415) 621-6800

www.bdantiques.com

The French General

2009 Riverside Drive
Los Angeles, CA 90039
(323) 668-0488

www.frenchgeneral.com

Tail of the Yak

2632 Ashby Avenue
Berkeley, CA 94705
(510) 841-9891

Tinsel Trading Company

Trims, flowers, tassels, ribbons, appliques, jewelry, handmade paper, stationery items, gifts and more.

1 West 37th Street
New York, NY 10018
(212) 730-1030

www.tinseltrading.com

The Silk Trading Company

360 S. La Brea Avenue
Los Angeles, CA 90036
(323) 954-9280

www.silktrading.com

FAVORITE ARTISANS:

Laurie Callaway

Garden Design

LaurierCallaway@aol.com

Melissa Neufeld

Craft Artist

NeufeldML@earthlink.net

Ingrid Erickson

Designer and Custom Seamstress

ingridericsondesigns@gmail.com

Pascual's Upholstery

Custom Furniture and Upholstery

255 Kansas Street Suite 200
San Francisco, CA 94103
(415) 255-7365

pascualsfurniture@sbcglobal.net

ABOUT
THE AUTHOR

DENA FISHBEIN is the artist and creative force behind Dena Designs, Inc. Her many products—including bedding, textiles, gifts, accessories, apparel, and greeting cards—are sold by major retailers, among them Neiman Marcus, Horchow, Dillards, Belk, Barnes & Noble, Bed, Bath & Beyond, Le Bon Marche in Paris, and other leading retailers around the world. Dena's media background includes hosting the series *Embellish This!* on the DIY cable network and writing a monthly newspaper column for Scripps Howard. Dena lives in Lafayette, California, with her family.

ACKNOWLEDGMENTS

To Danny, the love of my life since I was fifteen.

To Dad, the most supportive, wonderful father imaginable. Truly.
And to Mom—you are one cool babe. I love you both
so much.

To David, Rachel, and Lisa. Chicken, Chicken of the Sea,
and Chickster. I love you all more than Miles.

To my agent, Alex Meisel, who is a rockstar and a mensch.

To Julia, my forever friend.

To the Divas: Kathleen, Sheila, Anne, Melissa, Brenda, and Tina,
who are all geniuses and like sisters to me.

Thank you to Ingrid Erickson, for being both talented and
delightful. What planet did you say you were from?

To Laurie Calloway, our wonderful garden designer who always
brings me flowers.

To Heidi, such a superstar; Katrina, our office fairy (and
secret shanker); and darling Zoe.

You are all the best, and I'm so lucky to have you in my life.
Thank you.

Library of Congress Cataloging-in-
Publication Data
The painted home by Dena.
    p. cm.
  ISBN 978-1-58479-962-7
1. House furnishings. 2. Machine
sewing. I. Dena Designs.
  TT387.P365 2012
  646.2'044—dc23
                                    2011049252
Editor: Wesley Royce
Designer: LeAnna Weller Smith
Production Manager: Tina Cameron

The text of this book was composed in
ATSackers Gothic, Copperplate Gothic,
Gotham, and Miller.

Printed and bound in China

10 9 8 7 6 5 4 3 2

ABRAMS
THE ART OF BOOKS SINCE 1949

115 West 18th Street
New York, NY 10011
www.abramsbooks.com